Tell me about

The Oceans

Published by the United Nations Educational,
Scientific and Cultural Organization (UNESCO),
7, place de Fontenoy, 75352 Paris 07 SP, France.

The designations employed and the presentation of material throughout this publication do-not imply the expression of any opinion whatsoever on the part of UNESCO concerning the legal status of any country, territory, city or area or of its authorities, or the delimitation of its frontiers or boundaries.

Original title: *Raconte-moi les océans*

Reprint 2005

© UNESCO, 2003, for the texts and photos

© Nouvelle Arche de Noé, 2003, for the layout and illustrations

ISBN UNESCO 92-3-103872-9

Illustrations: Pascale Collange
Layout: Franck Tournel
Printing: Ages Arti Grafiche, Turin

All rights reserved.
No part of this publication may be reproduced in any form or by any means without the-written permission of UNESCO Publishing.

www.unesco.org/publishing

Printed in Italy

TELL ME ABOUT
The Oceans

Patricia Chairopoulos
Translated by Linda Blake

UNESCO Publishing

Table of Contents

The oceans: a short introduction . . 6
    Their beginnings 7
    Salty water 7
    Ocean floors 7
    Geographic organization 10
    Winds and currents 11

The oceans: balancing our climate . . 13
    Oceans and world climate 13
    Oceans and carbon 14
    The Global Ocean Observing System 16

*Flora and fauna of
the world's oceans* 18
    Biological distribution of species 18
    Biodiversity 18
    Ecosystems 19
    Endangered species 20

Ocean resources 23
    Resources exploited today 23
    The oceans' new resources 25

Oceans and human beings 28
    Inventory 28
    *Urbanization and tourism:
    threats to the littoral** 31

Oceans and pollution 34
    Sources of pollution 34
    Long-term consequences 36
    *Humans are directly affected
    by-pollution* 37

Sustainable development 38
    Just what does this mean? 38
    *UNESCO and sustainable
    development* 41

Glossary 44

Useful addresses 47

The images we usually have of the oceans are often limited to waves breaking on the shore and washing golden beaches, fishing boats loaded with fish sailing under the sun, or violent storms raging at sea. But the oceans form an immense realm, covering three-quarters of our planet. They are an integral part of our lives yet remain unknown to us in many ways, full of mystery and invaluable treasures that are indispensable for life on Earth.

Poets, scientists, politicians, fishermen, businessmen, tourists, you and I – we are all attracted, for different reasons, by these vast, constantly moving stretches of water. One thing is certain however: while the oceans and seas fascinate us, we should also feel responsible for their protection.

For many years now, we have cared too little about this. We do not hesitate to exploit marine resources and allow dangerous cargo ships to cross the oceans. More and more buildings invade the seacoasts along our beaches. But worst of all, the seas have become the world's biggest rubbish dump. Yet seas and oceans are fragile and they don't have an unlimited capacity.

The truth is quite simple: life cannot exist without the oceans. If we expect too much of them, we may end up causing irreparable damage to our planet's ecosystem. We must therefore respect them and live in harmony with them. This means killing fewer whales and catching fewer fish. If treated properly, the oceans can bring us countless benefits. This book will take you on a voyage through this fascinating 'blue world', a world that is vital for us all.

Patricio A. Bernal

Executive Secretary

Intergovernmental Oceanographic Commission

The oceans: a short introduction

Did you know?

Among the colours that make up sunlight, blue penetrates deepest into water, giving the seas and oceans their blue colour.

The Earth is often called the 'blue planet'. Seen from space, it looks blue because of all the water on its surface. Three-quarters of the globe are covered with seas and oceans, representing 361 million square kilometres of salt water! The world's seas and oceans contain practically all the water on the planet, the rest is mostly fresh water stored in the form of ice in polar ice caps* and glaciers and river water.

The marine environment is vast, complex and hard to access. We don't know much about it and studying this milieu* is both costly and complicated. And yet the world's oceans play a vital role in the planetary environment; we must learn more about them in order to protect it.

'The world's oceans and adjacent seas and all the organic and inorganic natural resources they contain are indispensable to the survival of our planet as we know it today. Safeguarding* the air we breath, the water we drink, the food we eat and the climate we live in depends on the oceans.' This was the declaration made by UNESCO's Intergovernmental Oceanographic Commission (IOC) at the World Summit for Sustainable Development held in Johannesburg in September 2002.

Words followed by an asterisk (*) are explained in the Glossary, p. 44

💧 Their beginnings

How were the oceans created? In order to answer this, we must go back four and a half billion years to the earliest ages of the Earth. There were many active volcanoes at the time, spewing out thousands of tons of magma. This gooey, burning hot liquid rock contained enormous quantities of gas that created the Earth's first atmosphere*, known as the primitive atmosphere, and which was full of steam. With the cooling of the Earth, the water vapour condensed and became a liquid. Diluvian* rains fell to the ground and accumulated in the low-lying areas of the land, creating ponds and lakes and, little-by-little, the world's first seas and oceans. Over time the composition of these bodies of water changed, but not their quantity, which has always remained the same since the very beginning and represents one and a half billion cubic kilometres of water!

Did you know?

The salinity or proportion of salt in seawater varies in relation to geographic location. In-subtropical climates, rain is scarce and evaporation is very high because of the heat. Seawater is consequently saltier in these regions.

💧 Salty water

In the beginning, seawater was fresh water. During the hundreds of million years since seawater came into being it has been continually loaded with mineral salts and biological matter. These substances are carried by rivers and result from the decomposition of rocks beneath the sea and from gases that escape from the Earth's crust when volcanoes erupt.

💧 Ocean floors

Ocean floors are not flat but have highly contrasted reliefs*. Because the oceanic crust is cut up into pieces, ocean floors are mountainous and their shapes change. In places the

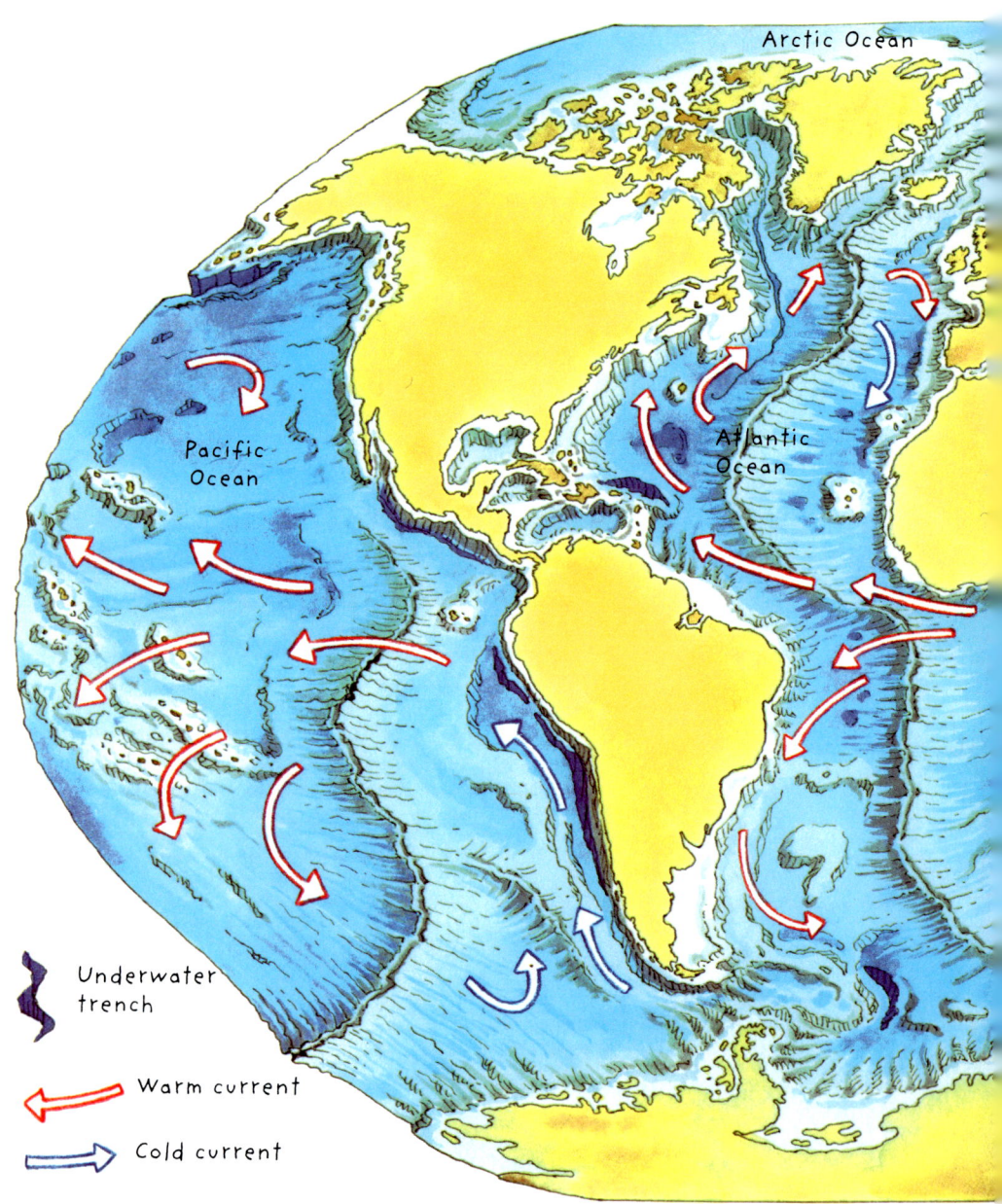

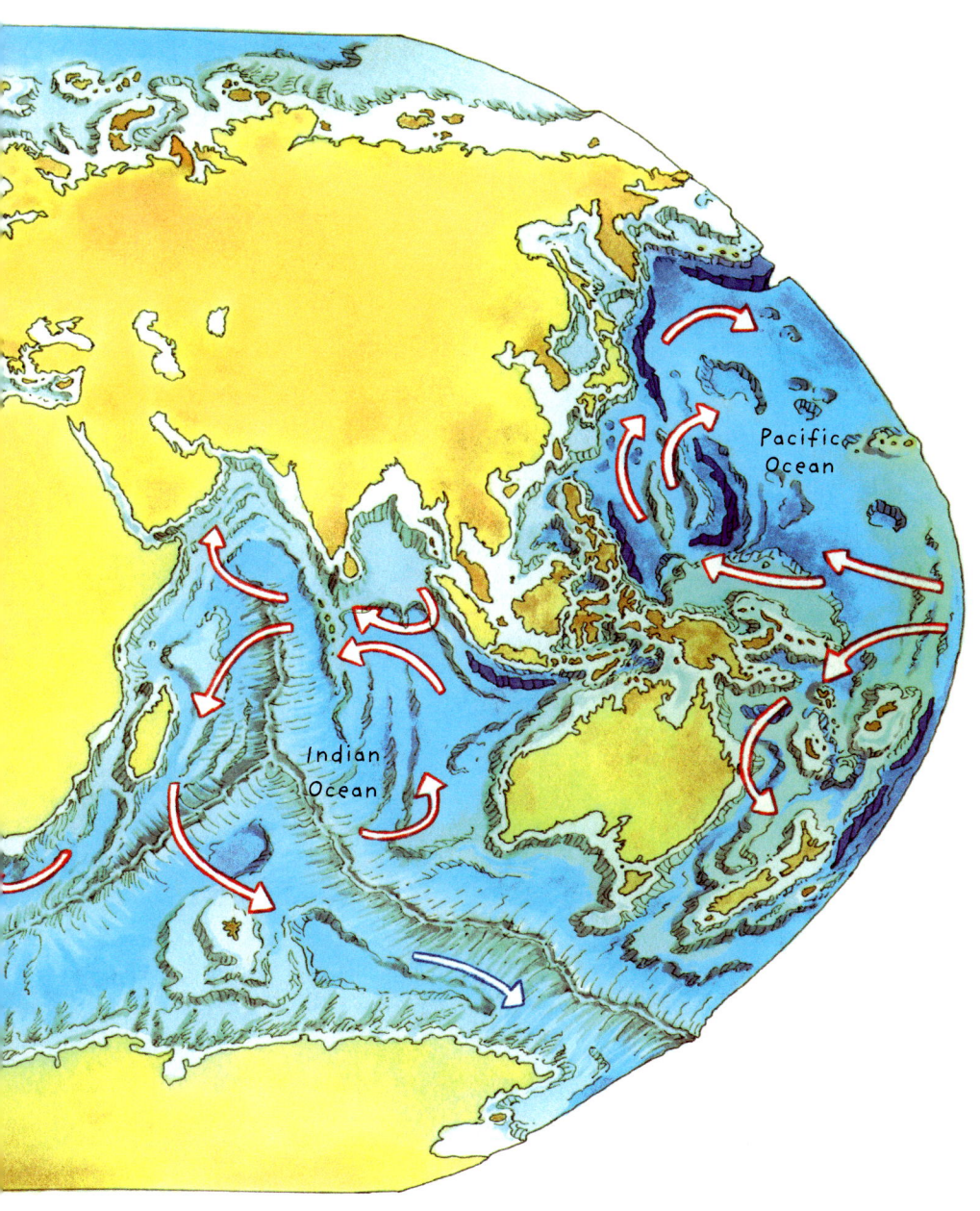

In some spots on Earth, the surface current close to the coast is replaced by cold water rich in nutrients that wells up from the depths. This phenomenon is called upwelling. We know of four major areas where upwelling occurs: these are principally located along the west coast of Africa. Fishing is intensive in these regions.

crust fissures and forms what is called the mid-oceanic ridges. Ranging from 1 to 4 kilometres in height and almost as wide, these enormous marine mountain chains stretch 60,000 kilometres over the globe like the seams of a baseball. Magma rich in minerals from the depths of the Earth spills out onto the ocean floor at these ridges, continually creating new oceanic crust. In some locations the magma spews out violently in the form of an undersea volcanic eruption. In other spots, the ocean floor disappears when a portion of oceanic crust slides into one of the deep-sea trenches, whose depth varies from 6,000 to 11,000 metres.

Just imagine for a second that the oceans have been drained. We would be able to see a landscape of mountain chains, plains, volcanoes and very deep valleys.

🌢 Geographic organization

Geographers distinguish three major oceans, the Pacific, the Atlantic and the Indian and two smaller ones, the Southern and Arctic Oceans. The Pacific Ocean is the biggest, containing half the total volume of the world's oceans, followed by the Atlantic and then the Indian Oceans. Although separated into three distinct basins* their waters meet in the southern hemisphere to form the

Southern Ocean surrounding Antarctica. The Arctic Ocean at the North Pole is covered with ice and despite its small size is still considered an ocean. Seas are smaller in size, are generally enclosed and are more or less separated from the oceans. Seas border continents and penetrate into them to a greater or lesser degree.

💧 *Winds and currents*

The sun heats the upper layer of the world's oceans to a depth of 20 to 30 metres. In doing so it causes the evaporation of enormous quantities of water, which escapes into the air in the form of water vapour. This transfer of heat between the ocean and the atmosphere, which is really a transfer of energy*, causes the air to stir, forming winds. Winds are responsible for creating some of the currents that keep ocean water moving. The three types of ocean currents are surface currents, density-driven or thermohaline currents and slope currents.

The action of the wind on the water's surface creates surface currents. But these don't move just any which way. Blowing along the equator, the trade winds create east-west currents. When they reach the continents these currents run along their edges. Due to the spinning of the earth, currents that meet continents are deviated to

Did you know?

The ocean currents and the-drain in your bathtub circulate water in the same direction because of the spinning of the earth. In the northern hemisphere water swirls clockwise; in the-southern hemisphere it swirls counter-clockwise!

the right in the northern hemisphere and to the left in the southern hemisphere (Coriolis effect), creating the Gulf Stream in the North Atlantic and the Australian current in the Pacific.

Density-driven or thermohaline currents are deep currents driven by differences in seawater density, caused by variations in salinity and temperature. These currents are very cold (around 0°C) and they are much slower than surface currents. It takes several centuries for them to circle the globe.

The least noticeable of the three currents are the slope currents. They can be explained by the fact that the ocean's surface is not flat but sloped 2 to 3 metres. This slope increases in the presence of atmospheric low-pressure systems and decreases in the presence of high-pressure systems. Currents are created to compensate for these differences in an attempt to make the sea level.

> ### CHAPTER 17 OF THE ACTION 21 PROGRAMME
> In 1992, governments from around the world met in Rio de Janeiro for the United Nations Conference on the Environment and Development. This marked the first debate on the question of how to satisfy current needs without harming those of future generations (sustainable development). The Conference drafted a very thick report called the Action 21 Programme; Chapter 17 is devoted in its entirety to the world's oceans, reminding us that the ocean is indispensable for life.

Greenhouse gases act like a transparent lid: they let the sun's rays through but keep the heat of the Earth from escaping into space. This is why our planet is inhabitable, but the more the greenhouse effect is enhanced, the warmer our planet becomes.

The oceans: balancing our climate

◆ Oceans and world climate

The world's oceans play an important role in regulating world climate. So much so that they have been referred to as weather's 'steering wheel'. They act in several ways. First of all, oceans store heat when it is too hot either during the summer or during the day and then release heat in another season or at night.

But oceans are not just storage tanks. They are also vehicles: currents carry heat in great quantities from hot regions to cold regions. And when the heat returns to the atmosphere, marine breezes push it towards the continents. This is why it is often warmer closer to the ocean than farther inland. The Gulf Stream, for instance, carries warm water from the tropics and warms up the west coast of Europe. This is the reason the climate in western Europe is much milder than in central Europe.

Rainfall is also directly linked to the ocean. The evaporation of seawater fills the air with water vapour and this creates clouds. The amount of evaporation controls cloud frequency and size. In the tropics evaporation is so great during the day that when the sun sets and the air cools down, storm clouds form and cause short and violent downpours.

Water evaporation and rainfall

Did you know?

Around 380,000-cubic kilometres (km³) of water evaporate from the surface of seas and oceans each year and-only one-quarter of this amount falls on the continents.

The carbon dioxide cycle

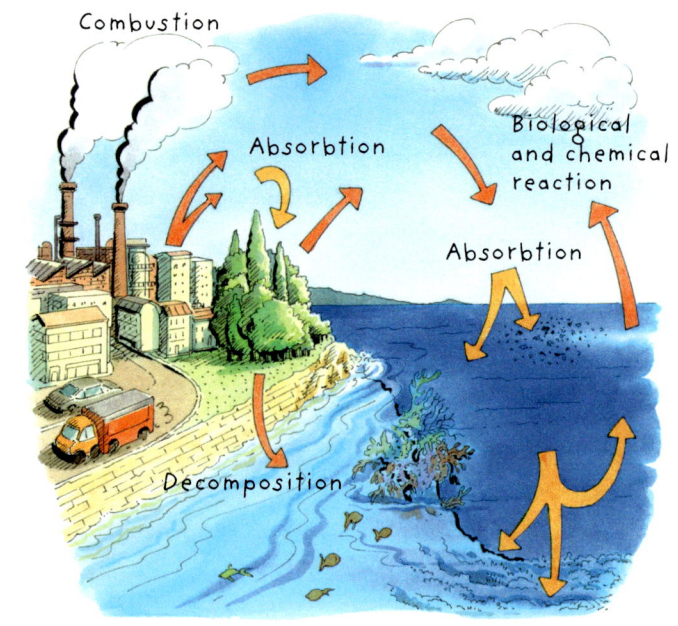

Did you know?

Each inhabitant of an industrialized country produces 5,000-kg of CO_2 per year in comparison to only 400 kg per inhabitant in developing countries.

The human production of carbon dioxide, primarily brought about by fuel combustion, is nearly 5 billion tons per year.

The relationship between the world's oceans and the atmosphere is extremely complex: winds and currents criss-cross and cause all kinds of climatic variations, from simple sea breezes to terrible hurricanes, which can be devastating. One such variation is called 'El Niño'. This large-scale oceanic phenomenon occurs in the Pacific and upsets the climate over that entire region of the globe, sometimes affecting even greater areas.

💧 Oceans and carbon

Another way oceans influence climate is by storing carbon. This atom* enters into the composition of many molecules*, including carbon dioxide (CO_2). This gas is naturally present in the atmosphere, but human activity (industry, automobile traffic and the burning of wood, coal, natural gas and fuel oil has increased its production. In addition to carbon dioxide, these activities also give off other gases, such as methane (produced by rice-growing and cattle-raising for instance) and 'ChloroFluoroCarbons' (CFCs). All these gases contribute to the enhanced greenhouse effect that is threatening to disturb the climate of our planet.

> **TRAPPING CARBON DIOXIDE IN THE WORLD'S OCEANS**
>
> Oceans are the biggest potential reservoir for storing the CO_2 produced by human activity and for keeping it from entering the atmosphere. This may be an effective way to reduce the consequences of too much CO_2. The IOC is closely monitoring initiatives aimed at developing a CO_2 trap. Two techniques are currently being tested: a) injecting this gas directly into the ocean bottom and b) helping plankton, which feed on CO_2, to grow in specific areas of the ocean (by adding iron dust). But where these 'traps' should be set, and above all, making sure that these techniques will not disturb oceanic ecosystems are major questions that must first be answered.

Due to global warming, the sea level is rising; if this continues, the sea level will be around one metre higher in 100 years. The Maldive Islands in the Indian Ocean will be wiped off the map.

Here again the world's oceans play an essential role because they naturally absorb great quantities of CO_2: approximately 18 billion tons per year. Algae consume part of this amount and the remainder falls to the sea floor. But this absorption capacity has its limits. In 100 to 200 years it will be saturated and will no longer be able to compensate for the CO_2 emissions caused by human activity.

The average temperature on earth is already rising. Without efforts to lower greenhouse gas emissions, experts predict an increase in temperature of from 2 to 5°C by the end of the twenty-first century.

◆ The Global Ocean Observing System

Improving understanding of the role the world's oceans play in climate change has become a priority for the IOC of UNESCO. Together with the World Meteorological Organization (WMO) and other bodies, the IOC set up the Global Ocean Observing System (GOOS) in 1985.

Little-by-little, an army of satellites, ships and buoys have been deployed to monitor the world's oceans. They record water temperature, colour and salinity, wave height, current velocity and wind speed at regular intervals. These data are then transferred to super computers on all the continents where they are input into digital models that are used by scientists to simulate the behaviour of great expanses of the high seas and

To obtain reliable meteorological forecasts that account for the role played by the oceans, the IOC and its Member States are setting afloat automatic buoys. These monitors travel with the ocean currents and take measurements on the oceans' surface and at different depths at regular intervals.
Data are then transmitted to receiver stations around the globe.

TOGA

An observation and research system has been set up in the tropical Pacific to forecast the El Niño phenomenon. It's called the TOGA programme. All the governments concerned contribute to this programme; they may use the data collected to try to lower the potential effect of either drought or flooding in relation to agriculture, the use of water, management of the fishing industry and all other activities that depend on atmospheric conditions.

More important still, the programme has developed models that scientists now use to forecast the coming of El Niño one year in advance.

> ### EL NIÑO
> 'El Niño' generally occurs around Christmas — its name in fact means 'the infant Jesus' — along the South American coasts of the Pacific. The phenomenon occurs with more or less intensity every three to four years. It is believed to be caused by changes in the circulation of the trade winds. Normally these winds blow from east to west, pushing warm surface water towards Indonesia and Australia, and allowing deeper, colder water to surface along the South American coast. But sometimes the trade winds are not very strong or even blow in the wrong direction. The warm water is driven towards South America and raises the temperature of the ocean. The result is the giving off of heat and humidity that provokes storms and torrential rains in normally very arid regions.

coastal regions in order to prepare forecasts. This is called 'operational oceanography'. The forecasts are available to be both public and private users. Weather services use them to forecast the weather and save lives, for example by identifying a hurricane in formation.

Did you know?

Some scientists estimate that the sea level rises by 2.5-mm per year due to global warming and that this could cause the flooding of inhabited zones and agricultural areas.

When El Niño occurs, Australia is subjected to drought, whereas the customarily dry regions of the eastern Pacific, such as Peru, are drenched with rain and completely flooded.

Flora and fauna of the world's oceans

> **Did you know?**
>
> The gigantic baleen whale feeds exclusively on tiny zooplankton.

💧 *Biological distribution of species*

Life flourishes everywhere in the oceans of the world. Algae, jellyfish, crustaceans, fish, cetaceans* and other marine animals live and proliferate. There are approximately 250,000 marine animal species in all. Most of them live in the upper part of the sea, down to a depth of a few hundred metres; they prefer coastal zones and also zones where upwelling occurs (where cold water rises from the deep). In fact, this is where seawater contains the most nutrients. Phytoplankton* thrive near the water's surface and provide food for all forms of life at the beginning of the marine food chain*: zooplankton*, then fish, molluscs, sea mammals and so on. Life is much less abundant on the high seas.

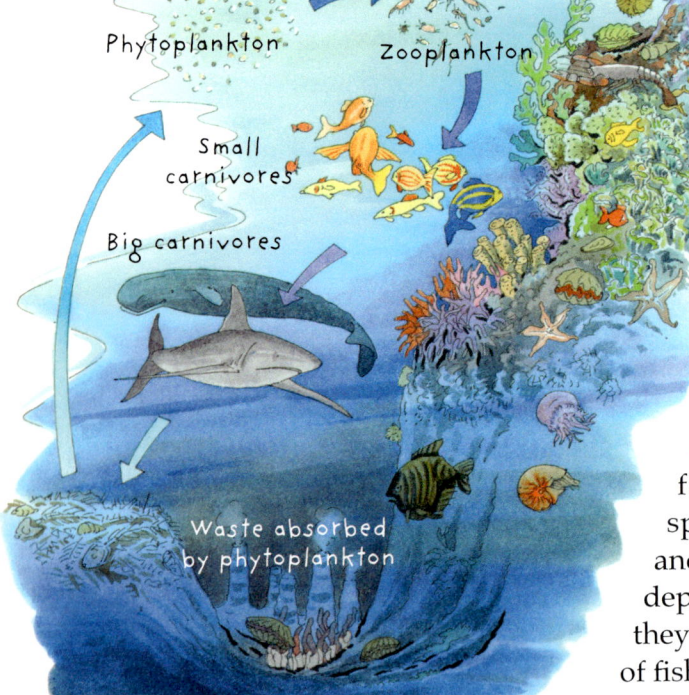

💧 *Biodiversity*

Marine species belong to two main categories:

💧 those that live on the ocean floor, are either fixed or mobile, are called 'benthic': mussels, scallops, crabs and sea urchins.

💧 those that live in waters far from the coast; these species are called 'pelagic' and are found at a few metres depth where there is still light; they include most of the species of fish consumed by humans.

These species swim in schools looking for food. Sharks and large marine mammals such as seals, dolphins and killer whales also live in this same area.

Not all the marine species have been identified. This is one of the goals of the Convention on biological diversity drafted in 1992 by the United Nations in partnership with IOC.

Did you know?

The sperm whale can dive to a depth of-over 1,500-metres and stay down there for more than an hour.

Fish waiting to dry, Portugal

💧 *Ecosystems*

An ecosystem* comprises both a natural milieu and the plants and animals that live in it. The ecosystems of the oceans are highly varied: coral reefs, abysses* (at a depth of over 2,500 metres) and the high seas. Some marine animals go from one ecosystem to another; this is the case for whales, which migrate from warm seas to cold seas. The ecosystems that are the richest in organic matter, and consequently in biodiversity are coastal waters, coral reefs and mangroves (mangrove forests plunge their roots into the sea).

Did you know?

6.5 million dolphins have perished over the last thirty years because of fishing nets.

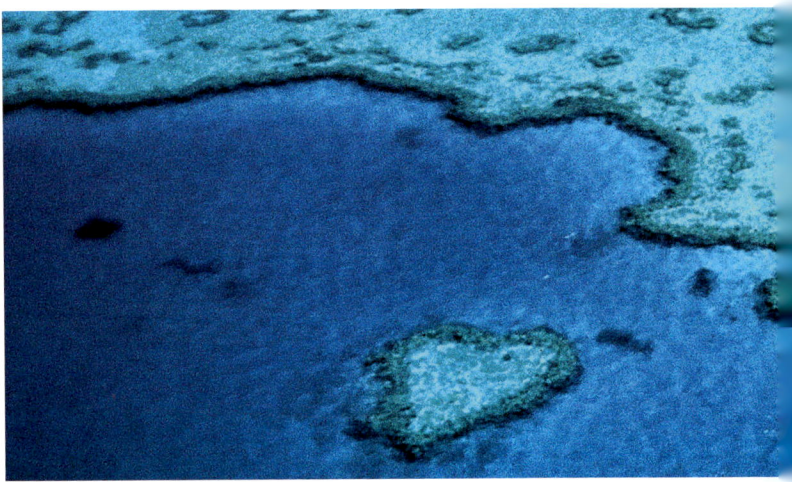

◦ *Endangered species*

Today, scientists estimate that 88 of the 126 marine mammal species are endangered, but the other marine species are not much better off. There are several reasons for this scarcity:

There are three good reasons to be alarmed by the growing scarcity of a species:
• it leads to an imbalance in the food chain, which disturbs the entire ecosystem;
• humans lose a potential source of income from fishing, which is vital to developing countries;
• it may possibly deprive humans of resources that are not yet known today (new drugs, new food sources, and so on).

◦ the increase in fishing caused by the human population explosion; this has led to over-intensive and poorly managed fishing practices. And this in turn caused the near extinction of some species in the 1970s, for example sea bream in France and Spain and anchovies in Peru;

◦ changes in the environment caused by pollution, the development/re-organization of some rivers (disturbing the migration of eels and salmon) and the over-exploitation of some ecosystems;

◦ the hunting down of large animal species over several centuries, with whales heading the list. Protected today, these species still risk

Coral reefs are among the richest and most beautiful ecosystems found on our planet. They are also among the most fragile. In the 1980s, many were affected by coral bleaching, an epidemic probably caused by pollution and the heating up of ocean waters. They have also been the victims of coral hunting and dynamiting to catch fish. The result: 70 per cent of coral reefs the world over are now endangered and a multitude of marine species along with them. The Philippines, Gulf of Guinea Islands, Sonde Islands, Mascareigne Islands, waters east of South Africa, northern part of the Indian Ocean, waters south of Japan, Taiwan and China, Cape Verde Islands, the western Caribbean Sea, Red Sea and the Gulf of Aden are the long list of zones where the risk of extinction is the greatest. The IOC is helping the countries concerned to monitor their reefs around the clock and participates in training caretakers.

being killed by poachers or by the enormous nets used by fishing trawlers in the Pacific (refer to the section titled 'The oceans and human beings').

A protected species in France since 1972, the monk seal has rapidly disappeared from the coastline of the Mediterranean Sea. And in regions where it is still found, the monk seal is often the victim of human ignorance. During the gestation* period, females must leave the water; tourists that sight them struggling up the beach, think they are in

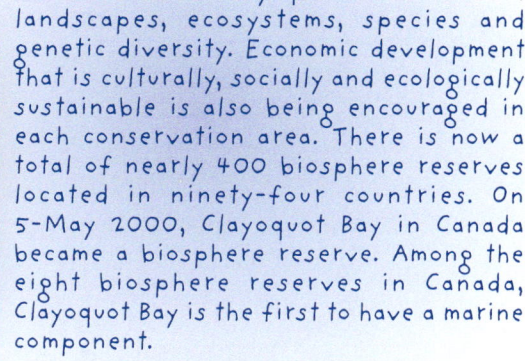

How can we protect biological diversity and meet the growing economic needs of humans at the same time? By creating biosphere reserves, says UNESCO. These areas simultaneously preserve natural landscapes, ecosystems, species and genetic diversity. Economic development that is culturally, socially and ecologically sustainable is also being encouraged in each conservation area. There is now a total of nearly 400 biosphere reserves located in ninety-four countries. On 5-May 2000, Clayoquot Bay in Canada became a biosphere reserve. Among the eight biosphere reserves in Canada, Clayoquot Bay is the first to have a marine component.

Among all the living species of the seas and oceans, so far, 100,000 molluscs, 50,000 algae, 25,000 fish, 5,000 sponges and around 150 marine mammals have been identified.

danger and throw them back into the water. Unfortunately this 'rescue mission' can simply kill both the mother and her baby.

Another focus of the Convention on biological diversity is concentrating on saving the planet's genetic pool*. We are unaware today what proportion marine species make up of the total number of species living on the Earth. We also know very little about the variety of plants and animals that live in the oceans' abysses.

Mangroves are over-exploited for their wood and purposely dried out to create more land for human exploitation. This-practice is-currently endangering many animal species.

Ocean resources

In addition to their biological resources, the world's oceans are rich in minerals and sources of energy that can be exploited by human beings.

🌢 *Resources exploited today*

🌢 Salt

Extracted from the sea since antiquity, salt was initially only used to preserve and season food. Today, it has become a raw material for the chemicals industry. Its scientific name is sodium chloride. How is it made? As a result of erosion*, the sodium in rocks is carried away by rivers to the sea. Seawater contains many elements such as magnesium and chlorine; sodium combines with chlorine to form sodium chloride. On average, seawater contains 35 grams of salt per kilogram of water. Seawater is evaporated in shallow basins in solar salt ponds to extract the salt. Solar salt ponds are located in regions where the climate is dry and warm, adjacent to the North and Mediterranean seas for example, and also in temperate zones, such as along the Atlantic coastline of France. One-third of the world's salt is extracted from seawater and the rest comes from many underground deposits, which are the remains of seas that no longer exist.

> **Did you know?**
>
> Salt content, or salinity is the total amount of dissolved solids contained in one kilogram of seawater.

Table salt is for the most part extracted from seawater. In Bolivia, seawater was trapped when the Andes were formed. Heated by the sun for thousands of years, the seawater evaporated, leaving enormous salt deposits.

> **Did you know?**
>
> 1 billion tons of-seawater contains 5 kilos of gold, 250 kilos of silver, 500-kilos of cobalt, 1,000-kilos of titanium, 2,000-kilos of nickel, 3,000 kilos of uranium, copper and tin and 10,000 kilos of zinc.

♦ Metals

Fifty years ago it was believed that mining manganese and other precious metals was going to become the new source of wealth to be taken from the oceans. The floors of the ocean deeps are strewn with multi-metal nodules – stones loaded with many metals. But since then we have learned how to extract these metals easily from the earth, and in great quantities. For the moment, seawater principally supplies us with bromine and magnesium. Bromine is produced from sea salt primarily in the United States, the Gulf of Mexico, Canada, France and Japan. Magnesium is obtained from the 'first stage waters' of solar salt ponds primarily in the Gulf of Mexico.

♦ Oil and gas

Oil and gas (hydrocarbons*) stored several hundred or several thousand metres beneath the ocean floor are extracted using costly, heavy machinery (platforms, hydrocarbon extraction systems). Two-thirds of the ocean's hydrocarbon deposits are located off the shores of Middle Eastern countries and are especially concentrated in the Persian Gulf. At present, marine hydrocarbon deposits supply 30-per cent of the total volume of oil produced worldwide and 10-per cent of the world's natural gas supply.

> *It is a well-known fact that hydrocarbons, whether taken from the sea or the ground, are at least partially responsible for global warming. Despite the growing concern of governments, it is unlikely that the use of hydrocarbons will decrease in the next few decades.*

● Fresh water

Desalination plants transform seawater into fresh, potable* water. Nowadays, some countries use this method to obtain the majority of their water supply.

There are two principal ways to remove salt from seawater: either by distilling it, whereby the water is heated until it evaporates and thus separates from the salt, or by filtering it, whereby the water is poured through very fine, highly perfected membranes. Even though distillation is the technique most widely employed today, filtering could become at least as profitable and as efficient in less than fifteen years.

Did you know?

1.4 billion persons living on the planet today don't have access to drinking water.

● The oceans' new resources

● Tidal energy

Strong tides are the source of considerable energy. This energy can be converted into electrical power at plants that harness tidal energy to drive turbines and generators. The first plant of this type was built in France in 1967. But this energy has not been developed as was initially hoped due to competition from nuclear power plants, which are less expensive, and the limited number of sites along the coast where tidal variations are sufficiently great to install tide-driven power plants.

● Wave energy

The energy created by waves is called mechanical energy; it can be harnessed by floating installations placed on the

After years and years of drought, many countries rely almost totally on the oceans for their freshwater supply. 12,500 desalination plants (the one above is in Israel) already ensure 1-per cent of the world's total production of potable water.

Did you know?

250 million clinical cases of intestinal flu and respiratory illnesses caused by bathing in contaminated waters are recorded each year.

water, or by shore installations. Plants of this type have been installed around the globe, and in particular in Japan, China, India, Norway and Great Britain. Converting this inexhaustible energy supply into electricity is pollution free. There is only one problem: the operating costs for these plants are still very high.

♦ Hydrothermal source

In 1977, the French deep-diving submersible *Cyana* discovered strange mineral structures that looked like termite mounds at a depth of 3,000 metres in the Pacific off the Mexican coast. These were hydrothermal sources, with temperatures that can exceed 350-°C. Shellfish and enormous worms were found living close by. Today, research into the ocean abysses is speeding forward; we know that bacteria* live without any problem in this hot environment completely deprived of light. How do they survive without any solar energy? We're just beginning to understand. Maybe some day these 'super-bacteria' will help us understand the origins of life itself.

◆ Drugs

The 200,000 species of invertebrates (fish, molluscs, crustaceans) and algae identified so far contain countless chemical substances whose composition is still unknown but which may be beneficial to health. The pharmaceutical industry has been studying them for the past forty years to discover whether they can be used to treat illnesses. Several of these substances are currently being tested for treating cancer.

Although considerable, the funds set aside by governments and private industry for marine observation and research to make advances in the field of pharmacology are often insufficient. The IOC helps governments by keeping them up to date on new techniques.

Intense research on the genetic material of marine species is currently being carried out by-the pharmaceutical and biotechnology industries. This research is leading to many discoveries and new products.

Oceans and human beings

💧 Inventory

The fact that there are 40-million fishermen in the world bears witness to one of the riches of humanity. The oceans' bounty is one of our last natural sources of food.

More than half the world's inhabitants live near seacoasts today at a distance of less than 200 kilometres from the water. In 2025, this will be the case for more than three-quarters of the world population, in other words for 6.3-billion persons! Most of them don't live in seaside resorts but are concentrated in enormous cities (metropolises) built on the coast. These city dwellers are often faced with poverty and some of them have less than two US dollars a day to live on.

If so many people crowd next to the shore it's because that's where the resources needed to sustain life are found in other words primarily fishing. But this poses a major problem because as the world population continues to grow and is concentrated in coastal areas it will increasingly depend on ocean resources.

> UNESCO's proposals for sustainable development and for lowering poverty in the coming decade, emphasis that both an economically viable way of life and the riches of the ocean must be made accessible to all, as well as an environment that is safer and healthier for coastal populations.

💧 Fishing, a vital food source

Fishing is the most widespread economic activity of the world's oceans. If fishing practices were better controlled this industry could feed more people and provide more jobs, especially in developing countries. But today, most fishing zones are being fished out. This is not surprising: 90 million tons of fish are caught each year! To arrive at this figure, fishermen haul in fish of-any size and any age, including the

very young, and those during their reproductive phase. Species don't have enough time to reproduce and their populations decrease more and more each year.

Industrial fishing techniques can be held responsible for overfishing and they also harm coastal fisheries. Poorly equipped, local fishermen work the waters close to the shoreline where the fish, which are victims of both overfishing and higher concentrations of pollution than in the open sea, are becoming increasingly scarce. In the southern part of the globe the inhabitants of many fishing villages have barely enough fish to eat. It is consequently nearly impossible for them to sell their catch.

Did you know?

Today, one in four shrimps and 80 per cent of mussels come from fish farms.

◆ The ravages of industrial fishing

In Europe, 'tangle drift nets' several kilometres in length wreck havoc* in the North Sea, the Atlantic and the Mediterranean. Weighted down at the bottom and held up by buoys at the top, these nets position themselves vertically beneath the surface of the water. They are allowed to drift with the currents and winds waiting for fish to be caught up in them. Sometimes they are attached at one end to a ship to 'herd' species towards the coast from the open sea. These nets are immense and much too long! Salmon is fished in the Baltic Sea with nets over 2-km long. The European Union voted to totally prohibit the use of tangle drift nets in Community waters as of 1 January 2002.

Factory ships are enormous 'fishing machines' (catching up to 1,000 tons per day). They rake the oceans, dragging enormous nets behind them (trawls or dragnets), freeze the fish that are deemed to have commercial value and throw the rest, most of which are condemned to die, overboard.

29

Fishing is one of the last natural food resources

Industrial fishing techniques are devastating. Fishermen not only haul in the species they're looking for but net other fish they don't want. They throw most of them – either dead or dying – back into the sea. Some of these are endangered species. Between 27 and 35 million tons of fish are 'wasted' in this way, meaning nearly one-third of all those that are caught! The FAO (Food and Agriculture Organization) of the United Nations has sounded the alarm. It estimates that the majority of fish stocks* are being overexploited and that the number of industrial fishing vessels must be lowered by one-quarter to return to the levels of abundance and catches of the 1970s.

Some States have already adopted measures forbidding or limiting the right to throw away fish at sea, primarily Iceland, Namibia, Norway and New Zealand. There are ways to fish only those species desired, but the techniques are not as profitable. But without resorting to selective fishing, net sizes could easily be reduced.

CONTROL MEASURES

To manage ocean resources, the United Nations Convention on the Law of the Sea, also known as the Montego Bay Declaration was signed in 1982 and ratified by 130 States. The Declaration, which came into force twelve years later, set up exclusive economic zones (EEZ) giving coastal States the exclusive fishing rights to all that the oceans contain within a 370-kilometre (200 nautical miles) limit from their coasts. Of course the States have also undertaken to protect and exploit the biological resources* of the high seas in such a way that sustainability is ensured. How is this accomplished? By encouraging fisheries to use selective fishing techniques that reduce waste to a minimum during hauls, by monitoring fishing operations, by protecting and restocking marine species endangered by extinction, and by preserving ecologically vulnerable zones. The IOC has also suggested creating protected areas on the high seas in international waters, but many countries are opposed to this idea.

In the waters of the open sea off France, nearly fourteen of the 350 fish species inventoried, such as the hake, are threatened with extinction due to overfishing.

IS AQUACULTURE A SOLUTION?

In use especially in Asia since the 1960s, commercial fish farms not only raise fish but also molluscs, crustaceans and algae.

Aquaculture may help provide a solution to the over-exploitation of fish stocks and the world population explosion. Many regions of the world already count on fish farms for food. But this method of breeding poses many problems for the environment. It is the first to be hit by pollution, especially if it is practiced close to cities, such as Hong Kong, and furthermore, this technique is itself very aggressive toward the environment. Fish farming pollutes because it discharges organic matter* and antibiotics into the water, and the construction of ponds or basins also destroys coastlines. This is the case for mangroves that have been converted into fish nurseries for commercial fish farming.

💧 Urbanization and tourism: threats to the littoral*

In both industrialized countries and developing countries, such as Brazil, urban growth along the coast has reached its limits. In Europe, the Mediterranean shoreline is covered with constructions over hundreds and hundreds of kilometres, completely blocking the landscape. The sandy soil settles with the weight of buildings and must be held in place by enormous concrete embankments in some locations. Many cities built below sea level are sinking. Both financial and technical means are needed to keep this from happening; means that developing cities do

Did you know?

The Mediterranean represents, by itself, about one-third of the world's tourism industry.

> **MAIN SPECIES FISHED IN THE WORLD**
> Peruvian anchovy
> Jack mackerel
> Alaskan pollack
> Atlantic herring
> Skipjack tuna
> Pacific herring
> South American pilchard
> Sea scallops
> Codfish
> Sabre or scabbard fish
> Sardine
> Yellowfin tuna
> Eastern, American or Atlantic oyster

not possess. Another major problem is sewage water, which is discharged into the sea along the coast, endangering all marine organisms.

To this must be added the massive influx of tourists and with them the construction of hotels in the dunes and beach 'renovation'. Around 100 million tourists congregate on the shores of the Mediterranean every year. And if this trend continues, there may be three to four times more by 2025. This sudden population explosion causes much harm to the marine environment, but tourism also boosts the fragile economies* of many countries. Since tourism is largely dependent on the quality of the environment, public authorities and private industry must ensure that the environment is safeguarded.

Life along the littoral is sometimes harmed by natural causes, for example by flooding following violent storms. The IOC actively promotes the forecasting and continuous monitoring of natural catastrophes that ocean forces sometimes let loose. These are often the result of the non-stop, heedless over-development of vulnerable coastal areas.

Human activity also includes the construction of dams on rivers and the destruction of mangroves to make room to grow timber commercially. These practices not only endanger the fragile balance of the marine ecosystem but the human beings who depend on it as well.

Human beings have lived for thousands of years on the world's seacoasts, drawn by the abundance of food and a milder climate than farther inland. But by living on the littoral and polluting it, they also endanger coastal areas and the ocean itself.

COAST PROTECTION PROGRAMME

Shallow coastal waters are important for marine ecology. They offer food and shelter for a large number of the fish we eat and provide space for the booming aquacole industry. This is why the IOC set up in 1997 a programme devoted to management of the coastal environment and coastal activities. The programme has several objectives: to reinforce the continual surveillance of the coastal milieu, share knowledge and information concerning this milieu that may be of help in resolving problems in the years to come, and help local authorities implement good practices. These actions are conducted by the governments concerned. Protecting coastal zones was one of the priorities discussed at the World Summit for Sustainable Development that took place in Johannesburg in September 2002.

Oceans and pollution

◆ Sources of pollution

Did you know?

The mussel stores pollutants and consequently serves as a means for checking pollution levels in coastal areas.

For a long time humans believed that the immensity of the oceans could absorb waste without any consequences. We now know that everything we throw into the ocean modifies its equilibrium: nothing is lost. Oil spills, the proliferation of algae in the Mediterranean, the disappearance of marine species. . . . We are aware today of the harm caused by pollution, which comes from two main sources.

Pollution from the continents represents 70 per cent of marine pollution. Sewage water, industrial waste (metals and phosphates), chemical waste, plastic, waters loaded with pesticides and fertilizers. Once they've been used for crops, fertilizers are carried by run-off to rivers, which then transport them to the sea.

The second main source is pollution resulting from maritime transport, and from oil transport in particular. Everyone knows about oil tanker accidents – *Erika* and *Prestige* being the most recent – but offshore oil rigs also cause the sadly famous 'oil spills'. Soiled beaches, oil-smeared birds, uneatable fish and shellfish: the damage they cause is horrendous. But on a worldwide scale, there is a far more serious form of pollution than oil spills from tanker accidents, and that is the deliberate discharge of oil, which as a result constantly degrades the marine environment. The principal guilty parties are the oil tankers that empty their cargo

> ### TARGETING POLLUTION
> In 1995, 108 governments and the European Commission working within the scope of the United Nations adopted the 'Programme of world action for the protection of marine environments against pollution caused by terrestrial activities'. All of these countries are trying to lower the emission of pollutants at their source, being aware that most pollution originates on land (is of terrestrial origin). A few of the ways this is accomplished are: by improving technical processes and closely monitoring industrial discharges; by limiting, in vulnerable zones such as Brittany in France, the use of fertilizers responsible for the proliferation of microscopic algae; and by building or improving wastewater treatment plants. These countries are also striving to improve human habitats in coastal areas, and to develop the coastline while respecting its natural features.

into the sea. This iscalled 'degassing' (degasification). Despite the creation of surveillance systems and the many measures taken to prohibit this practice, oil tankers are not always very scrupulous* and degas on the high seas clandestinely*. In all, approximately 600,000 tons of hydrocarbons are discharged into the oceans every single year! A large part of it is 'digested' by them: oil dissolves slowly in water and falls to the deeps to never rise again. But that doesn't keep it from seriously harming marine fauna, and this in turn diminishes the resources of developing countries, which are very dependent on ocean products.

Biodegradable?

2 months | 2 months | 5 to 10 years | 100 years | 100 to 500 years

In addition to hydrocarbons other aggressive pollutants also contaminate the oceans, notably waste from chemical products transported by ship that industrialized countries do not want to dispose of themselves. The result is that this cargo is sent to far away countries that are less strict about regulations, often to parts of Africa or South America. Thus, these are the places that are the most exposed to pollution hazards.

Did you know?

90 per cent of the toxic products discharged into the oceans pollute coastal waters, the very spot where humans exploit marine resources the most.

◆ Long-term consequences

All these pollutants have harmful effects on both the natural milieu and on humans. Some, like the famous insecticide DDT, stay in the water for years and accumulate in marine plants and animals. One of its effects is to weaken the natural defences of animals, which consequently become much more vulnerable to infectious diseases. Agricultural fertilizers deposited in the sea are responsible for the development of specific microscopic red and green algae. The algae proliferate and form a sheet 1 to 2 metres thick on the surface of the water. Because they are major consumers of oxygen, they end up asphyxiating* the shellfish and fish that live underneath. According to an IOC report, there is a 70,000 km² zone in the Baltic Sea where all forms of animal life have disappeared. Another consequence is that humans are simultaneously deprived of precious food sources.

♦ Humans are directly affected by pollution

The type of pollution that is most threatening to human beings is the discharge of sewage water. First it contaminates bathers, then fish and shellfish, and those who eat them in turn. Cholera and hepatitis epidemics caused through-eating contaminated food are becoming a frequent occurrence, especially in Latin America, around the Mediterranean and in Southeast Asia.

Just having a swim in polluted water is far from being harmless. According to the World Health Organization (WHO), this is the cause of nearly 250 million cases of intestinal flu each year as well as of respiratory illnesses. Generally speaking, one bather out of twenty risks becoming ill after taking a dip in the sea!

Did you know?

1 billion tons of oil is transported over the seas of the world every year.

SAILING PLASTIC

Each year several hundred kilos of solid waste wash up per kilometre of coast. Discharged into the sea by rivers or set adrift by boats, there is more of this waste all the time. Plastic comprises two-thirds of it. Floating over very long distances without deteriorating, plastic causes much damage to the marine ecosystem. Plastic bags are responsible in particular for smothering or strangling marine animals such as turtles, cetaceans and tuna, all of which confuse them with food.

Sustainable development

> **Did you know?**
>
> Two-thirds of all fish hauled in are caught in the Pacific.

💧 Just what does this mean?

Sustainable development is a way of meeting the needs of present day generations without compromising the capacity of future generations to meet their needs, for instance by improving the quality of water and the environment, by minimizing differences in the standard of living throughout the world, and by changing certain ways of living and consuming.

UNESCO is helping to open up an avenue of sustainable development focused on human beings and based on respecting the rights of humans and democratic principles, on solidarity, dignity, sharing and equality.

House torn from its foundations during a hurricane caused by El Niño, Honduras.

National Centre for Oceanographic Research at Nosy Bé, Madagascar.

💧 Three key dates

1987. The Brundtland Commission defined for the first time the concept of sustainable development before the United Nations.

1992. Governments met in Rio de Janeiro (Brazil) for the first Earth Summit (United Nations Conference on the Environment and Development). The summit focused on the key question of how to reconcile the demands of the present day with expectations for the future. There were many debates and alarming observations concerning the current state of our planet and the likely evolution of living conditions. To set the problems aright, more than 150 countries worked on a common programme for the twenty-first century, called the 'Action 21 Programme'. Since then this Programme has served as the basis for measuring the progress of the made in change in question.

Did you know?

A single super-tanker can transport as much as 400,000 tons of oil.

2002. From 26 August through to 4 September in Johannesburg, South Africa, 129 States, including some 100 Chiefs of State and 60,000 delegates, met under the aegis* of the United Nations for the World Summit on Sustainable Development, also called 'Rio +10'. Participants reported on both the progress made and failures since Rio, and on the projects that are needed right now. Despite the reluctance of rich countries to commit to figures and dates, this second Earth Summit accomplished at least two objectives:

> ### YEAR OF THE OCEAN
> The United Nations declared 1998 the 'Year of the Ocean'. The focus was on everything that the ocean represents for our existence, day-to-day lives, culture, and political and economic activity. The year ended with the drafting of an Ocean Charter translated into twenty languages and signed by millions of citizens around the globe. The Charter recognises the importance of the world's oceans and the need for co-operative action to tackle the problems they now face.

it made a collective decision to lower greenhouse gas emissions by 5.2 per cent within the next 10 years, and many States became aware of the urgency of remedying the ills of our planet.

Did you know?

Subsequent to extensive urban growth in the 1970s, Brazilian cities such as Sao Paulo and its surrounding areas still have major air and water pollution problems. Their beaches are suffering today because the most polluting industries have been relocated on the littoral.

◆ Chapter 17 of the Action 21 Programme

Healthy oceans and coastal regions are vital to sustainable development and poverty reduction. This is why, as mentioned earlier, the Action 21 Programme has an entire chapter devoted to the world's oceans. Their well-being is essential to the survival of living things and to the cultural, social and economic prosperity of human populations. To safeguard our survival or re-establish it we must learn how to manage the world's oceans and coastlines, basing our decisions on scientific knowledge. This concerns all the countries of the world because:

◆ one country alone cannot study and monitor the world's oceans on a continuous basis but it should at least be able to tackle the problems that touch its littoral;

💧 all countries depend either directly or indirectly on the world's oceans for survival and each must thus assume responsibility for its current condition. In addition, countries for which the economy and living conditions depend directly on the ocean must be provided with the means to solve problems on the local level.

💧 UNESCO and sustainable development

Over the past ten years, UNESCO has contributed a great deal to the sustainable development of the world's oceans through the IOC, the only organization in the United Nations system specialised in oceanography. The IOC doesn't work alone of course, but with many partners, such as other specialist institutions of the United Nations, various bodies, research institutes and laboratories.

Much progress has already been made on many projects, such as research on ocean climate and on climate variations over the long term; creation of the GOOS; improvement of interchange and distribution mechanisms for oceanographic data and information; the setting up of an integrated management programme for coastal areas; improving the comprehension of oceanic processes and of the impacts of human activity on the marine environment, and strengthening oceanography departments and the research capacities of developing countries.

Did you know?

35,000 industrial fishing vessels plough the seas.

Because of the waste discharged by factories installed on the seashore up to 20 per cent of fish in some areas of the North Sea are not fit for consumption.

The paper industry is one of the biggest polluters.

Over the next few years, the IOC's overriding goal will be to give more weight to scientific findings in making management decisions, and to raise the general public's awareness of the importance of the world's oceans and coastal areas for sustainable development and the future of humanity.

> ### THE IOC
>
> The IOC was created in 1960 under the aegis of UNESCO to help governments resolve problems linked to the world's oceans and coastal areas. The Commission works in two ways:
> - it pools knowledge, data and techniques and makes them available to everyone;
> - it carries out a common programme in different countries.
>
> The overriding priority of the IOC is to increase the capacity of developing countries so they may effectively participate in raising and answering questions related to the marine environment on equal footing with other countries, and receive all the benefits.
>
> Since 1999, the IOC has a new charter and 129 member States currently belong to the Commission. Each holds a seat at the Assembly, which meets every two years.

Certain animals cannot survive if ocean pollution is too high. The blue-footed booby can now only be found in the Galapagos and on the Isla de la Plata, Equator.

The temperamental nature of the oceans is an important factor in a considerable number of critical environmental situations.

'As they exist today the world's oceans are a vital element of the planetary environment in which we thrive; it is our job to find out how robust or fragile this relationship is. The world's oceans have sustained living marine organisms for thousands of years. We must now handle this invaluable resource with care to ensure that we do not destroy its capacity to sustain life through our ignorance of the marine environment and its ecology.' (conclusion of the IOC document, *One Planet, One Ocean* published for the World Summit on Sustainable Development held in 2002).

During the World Conference on Oceans and Coastal Zones held in December 2001, the conference co-presidents declared: 'We have good reason to be concerned about the well-being of the world's oceans and coastal areas. The Conference participants agree that the situation has become critical and requires immediate action on the part of States and major intergovernmental organizations.'

Did you know?

Up to the present time only 1.5 million species have been identified out of tens of millions of species that probably live on our planet.

In the ocean deep more than 2,500 metres down, life-sustaining conditions are extreme. There is very little oxygen, no light and temperatures are high in certain locations. And yet we have recently found crabs and giant worms in these deep, dark waters that have adapted to this inhospitable environment. Further investigations of this very unusual ecosystem will very likely lead to the discovery of plant and animal species as yet unknown.

Glossary

Abyss: gorge or fissure of immeasurable depth

Aegis: (under the aegis of) under the patronage of, supported by

Asphyxiating: suffocating

Atmosphere: gaseous envelope several hundred kilometres thick that surrounds the earth

Atom: smallest particle of a chemical element representing the smallest quantity of the element that can be combined with other elements

Bacteria: microscopic, single-cell beings that are neither plant nor animal and that act during fermentation and putrefaction to transform living matter into gases and other inert substances. Some bacteria give off toxic substances capable of causing infectious diseases in animals and humans

Biological resources: all plant and animal species living in a natural milieu, such as the oceans

Cetaceans: giant mammals (animals giving live birth), such as whales and dolphins that live in the water and that have lungs, breathing air for oxygen

Clandestinely: in a secret and concealed manner

Diluvian: of or connected with a deluge or very heavy rainfall

Economy: human activity aimed either directly or indirectly at obtaining wealth (material goods and personal services) to satisfy human needs and desires

Ecosystem: the set of interactions that tie living organisms to their physical and chemical environment

Energy: the force needed to do work. Energy can be of several types: mechanical, chemical or electrical

Erosion: the wearing away of rocks caused by the action of wind and water

Food chain: each of its links corresponds to the relationship between the one that eats and the one that is eaten. In the ocean the food chain starts with plankton, which are fed upon by small carnivorous animals, themselves food for larger fish and marine mammals

Genetic pool: the set of genes of all living species

Gestation: period between conception and birth when a baby is carried by its mother

Hydrocarbons: long molecules composed of chains of carbon and hydrogen atoms; depending on the number of carbon atoms, hydrocarbons are primarily oil and gas (methane, for instance)

Ice cap: ice that permanently covers land masses in polar regions (Greenland and Antarctica)

Littoral: a coastal or shore region

Milieu: an environment or surroundings

Molecule: the simplest unit of a chemical compound that can exist, consisting of two or more atoms held together by chemical bonds

Ocean basin: depression in the earth's crust that filled with water when the oceans were created

Organic: of, relating to or derived from living plants and animals; also any product derived from plants and animals containing carbon

Organic matter: composed of molecules rich in carbon, hydrogen, oxygen and nitrogen atoms and characterizing living beings; in contrast to inorganic (mineral) matter, organic matter changes over time and in relation to environmental changes caused by microbes, chemical substances, physical phenomena, for example

Phytoplankton: plant plankton

Plankton: generally microscopic drifting or floating organic life; plankton are the beginning of the oceanic food chain; phytoplankton is composed of microscopic algae and zooplankton of tiny animals, especially minute crustaceans

Potable: drinkable

Relief: lay of the land showing elevations and depressions or variations in level or altitude

Safeguard: to guard or protect

Scrupulous: careful to avoid doing wrong; conscientious; the opposite of unscrupulous

Stock: population of fish or other animals either fished, hunted or raised by human beings, for example the stock of hake in the Gulf of Gascogne off the coast of France

Wreck havoc: to cause disaster; destruction; devastation

Zooplankton: animal plankton

Useful addresses

UNESCO
7, place de Fontenoy
75732 Paris 07 SP, France

Internet

UNESCO
http://www.unesco.org

Intergovernmental Oceanographic Commission (IOC)
http://www.ioc.unesco.org/iocweb/default.htm

Associated Schools Projects (ASP)
UNESCO's Associated Schools Project gathers together thousands of-educational institutions across the world. Associated Schools commit to-promoting the ideals of the Organization by conducting pilot projects, in-particular in the field of the environment.
http://www.unesco.org/education/asp/

French Research Institute for Exploitation of the Sea
http://www.ifremer.fr/anglais/

European Environment Agency
http://www.eea.eu.int

In the same collection:
"Tell me about… Explaining..."

UNESCO,
WORLD HERITAGE,
BIOSPHERE RESERVES,
THE CLIMATE.

Photos © UNESCO

Y. Arthus-Bertrand (pp. 15, 20-21), F. Charaffi (p. 22/2),
M. Claude (p. 21/2), Fernandez (p. 10), I. Forbes (pp. 14, 24),
E. Frogé (pp. 12, 19, 41, 42), P. Fury/AREPI (p. 34), M. Ginies (pp. 17, 38, 43),
A. Jonquières (p. 23), Y. Latronche (p. 28), S. Le Nechet (p. 26),
M. Rapillard (p. 31), D. Roger (pp. 6, 11, 16, 30, 33/1-2, 37, 39),
N. Saunier (p. 25), A. Wheeler (pp. 22/1, 22/3)